Remembering
The Chicago World's Fair

Russell Lewis

TURNER
PUBLISHING COMPANY

The Horticulture, Choral, and Transportation buildings stand tall behind the intertwined pathways of the Wooded Island's Rose Garden.

Remembering
The Chicago World's Fair

Turner Publishing Company
www.turnerpublishing.com

Remembering The Chicago World's Fair

Library of Congress Control Number: 2011929755

ISBN: 978-159652-835-2

Printed in the United States of America

ISBN: 978-1-68336-890-8 (pbk.)

Contents

Landscape architect Frederick Law Olmsted directed workers to create the Lagoon by dredging low areas of Jackson Park and using the fill to raise terraces that would support the fair buildings.

ACKNOWLEDGMENTS

This book, *Remembering the Chicago World's Fair,* would not have been possible without the support and assistance of my colleagues at the Chicago History Museum. I am grateful to the staff of the Research Center, who helped with the logistics of retrieving, copying, and digitizing images from the collection. My thanks go to Debbie Vaughan, Michael Featherstone, Mathew Krc, and Benjamin Bertin. I am also indebted to the members of the Rights and Reproduction staff who guided me to various White City collections, gave me unfettered access to the images, and played a key role in the process of making digital files of the images in this book. Rob Medina, Bryan McDaniel, and especially Erin Tikovitsch were extremely helpful. Photographers John Alderson and Jay Crawford used the highest professional standards in their scanning and digital conversion efforts. Rosemary Adams lent her critical editorial eye to the text and improved both prose and grammar, and I am grateful to her for her kind assistance. Finally, Gary Johnson, President of the Chicago History Museum, has been supportive and encouraging of this book, and he has been an ongoing champion of the Museum's partnership with Turner Publishing. At Turner Publishing, I am grateful to the staff and to publisher Todd Bottorff for all of their efforts to make the publication of this book possible.

This book is dedicated to Joseph H. Levy, Jr., Life Trustee of the Chicago Historical Society
and extraordinary friend and supporter of the Chicago History Museum.

With the exception of touching up imperfections that have accrued over time and cropping where necessary, no changes have been made to the photographs. The focus and clarity of many photographs is limited to the technology and the ability of the photographer
at the time they were taken.

PREFACE

The World's Columbian Exposition of 1893, a commemoration of the anniversary of Christopher Columbus's arrival to America, was the most photographed event in the nineteenth century. Images of the Court of Honor, the Ferris wheel, and the Midway Plaisance remain fresh in our minds, providing critical documentation for historians and a visual record that satisfies the public's thirst to imagine the experience of visiting this world's fair. Equally important, fair organizers consciously used photography to create an official image of the fair and aggressively promote it. The fair's Department of Publicity and Promotion (the Columbian Exposition was the first world's fair to have a formal publicity operation), which operated under the able leadership of Moses P. Handy, flooded the nation with photographic images of the exposition. Taking advantage of the growing popularity of publishing halftone photographic images in newspapers and magazines, Handy brilliantly engineered a mass distribution of official photographic images that shaped Americans' perceptions of the White City and encouraged them to attend the exposition.

The Columbian Exposition was also the first world's fair to restrict photography and grant an exclusive license for event photography to one individual. Charles Dudley Arnold, commissioned by fair organizers to photographically document the construction of the fairgrounds, was granted, with his partner , Harlow D. Higinbotham, the exclusive rights for commercial photography on the fairgrounds. Amateur photographers, who had increased significantly in recent years thanks to the introduction of George Eastman's Kodak snapshot camera, and inexpensive film and film processing, were eager to make their own photographs of the fair. They were charged $2 per day for fairground use of a handheld camera that made images no larger than four by five inches; the Streets of Cairo concession on the Midway charged an additional $1 to photograph there. Because tripods were forbidden, amateur photographers resorted to ingenious solutions to steady their cameras—placing them on tabletops, clamping them to the backs of chairs, and using railings or ledges. This combination of official photographs and amateur snapshots provides a remarkable visual record of the World's Columbian Exposition that not only captures the scale and grandeur of the exposition grounds and structures but also documents the visitors' experiences and points-of-view.

The Chicago History Museum has one of the nation's richest collections of materials on the World's Columbian Exposition, and its extensive holdings of photographs are a key component of these remarkable documents and artifacts. Including both official views of the fair by C. D. Arnold, photographs by William Henry Jackson made for Daniel H. Burnham, portraits by James J. Gibson, and amateur snapshots (by both identified and unidentified photographers), the image collection provides a powerful reminder of the importance of this event in American history. However, the photographs gathered in this volume can give the reader only a hint of what visitors experienced in the White City. The scale of the fairgrounds, the amazing array of events and programs available each day, and the personal experiences of visitors make it impossible for any book to comprehensively document the Columbian Exposition as a place and as an event. While much of the fairgrounds is photographically documented in great detail, other parts are not, and thus despite all we know about the White City, complete knowledge about some aspects of the fair remain elusive and await future research.

Finally, this book builds on the wonderful body of scholarly works that first began in the 1970s and that have continued to mine this rich moment in Chicago's and America's history.

Grading the site of the Fine Arts Building proceeded more quickly than with other buildings because it was part of Lake Front Park, the north end of Jackson Park, which had already been improved.

BUILDING THE WHITE CITY

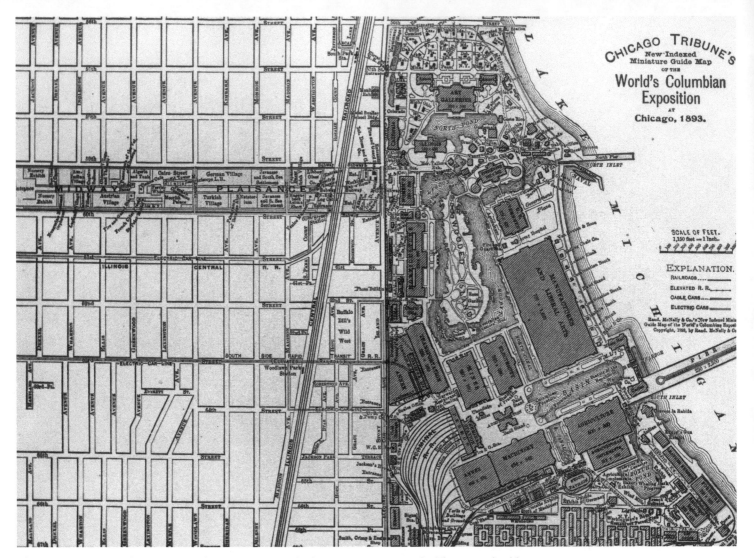

The exposition grounds encompassed 685 acres, just a little over one square mile. The major buildings were aligned with three major bodies of water: Lake Michigan, the Lagoon at Wooded Island, and the North Pond.

This faithful bird's-eye view reveals the scale of the fairgrounds and buildings spread across seven key areas: the Court of Honor, the Lagoon, government buildings, state buildings, the Midway Plaisance, the southeastern section, and the southwestern section.

This photograph of the Manufacturers and Liberal Arts Building site was taken in October 1891. Rather than eliminate the plentiful water on the site, Frederick Law Olmsted made it a main feature and theme of the exposition, establishing a network of basins, lagoons, canals, and ponds that linked the different parts of the grounds.

Work on the fairgrounds began in June 1891, with between 5,000 and 6,000 workers.

Construction began with the massive movement of earth and the grading and filling of land. By the end of construction, workers had moved more than 1.2 million cubic yards of earth, at a cost of $500,000.

Dredging to form the Lagoon was a priority during the initial phases of construction in August 1891.

By 1892, the skeletal silhouette of a city emerged in Jackson Park. This view north from the Agriculture Building across the Great Basin shows the Manufacturers and Liberal Arts Building, designed by George Post, and the dome of the Horticulture Building.

Looking west across the Great Basin are the Agriculture Building, left, the Administration Building, center, and the Electricity Building, right, under construction. The Administration Building was designed by prominent architect Richard Morris Hunt, also known for designing the Great Hall of the Metropolitan Museum of Art and the pedestal of the Statue of Liberty.

The interior of the Mines and Mining Building shows the structure's steel trusses. The ghostly image of the workers (left) gives a sense of the scale of the framework and the building.

The steel skeletal framing of the Electricity Building dominates the view looking east from the Mines and Mining Building, December 1891. Constructing the framing of the buildings was hazardous work, and progress was delayed by bad weather and strikes.

Constructing the Manufacturers and Liberal Arts Building was a Herculean task. The plaster classical facade masked the steel skeleton, which was the foundation of modern architectural and construction methods.

This suited man leans against the massive foot of one of the steel arches of the Manufacturers and Liberal Arts Building, March 26, 1892. Chicago's familiarity with steel-frame construction was a key factor in erecting the exposition structures quickly.

Wooden framing was constructed for the Golden Door of the Transportation Building. Architect Louis Sullivan designed the Transportation Building with modern elements and several colors, making the building stand out as the only structure of its kind in the White City.

The wooden framework of the Woman's Building is pictured on March 30, 1891. The Woman's Building, one of the first structures enclosed at the fair, was designed by 22-year-old Sophia Hayden, the first American woman to receive a degree in architecture. Hayden was paid a meager $1,000 to complete her design.

This view from the Wooded Island depicts exterior work on the plaster facade of the Horticulture Building.

This winter view of the western facade of the Woman's Building was recorded on February 12, 1893, a few months before the fair opened. The Italian Renaissance–style building housed 7,000 books provided by various states and countries.

Workers apply finishing touches to the loggia of the Machinery Building. The Administration Building is visible to the right. The $1.2 million Machinery Building contained the power plant for the entire fair.

Staff, which was first used on the exterior of buildings at the 1889 Paris world's fair, had the properties of plaster and cement and hardened into an ivory-like surface resembling marble. Workers used gelatin molds to make multiple copies of bas-relief panels.

This sculptural model was made for the Transportation Building. Artists did much of the modeling work for sculpture and ornamental pieces in the Forestry Building.

Charles Dudley Arnold photographed this model for a sculptural ornament for the Electricity Building, along with its sculptor, on August 27, 1891. C. D. Arnold was designated the official photographer of the exposition.

A full-scale replica of the U.S. Navy battleship *Illinois* was built of bricks and cement and was part of the Naval Pier exhibit near the North Pier.

The Ho-o-den or Phoenix Palace was a replica of the famous Ho-o-den temple, Nji, near Kyoto, Japan. Japanese government architect Kuri Masamichi designed the structure and shipped numbered parts to Chicago for assembly. Japanese craftsmen from Okura & Company reassembled it at the north end of the Wooded Island, and it was one of the few buildings allowed on the island.

A meeting takes place among the world's fair officials, including George R. Davis (standing), director general of the World's Columbian Commission; and Harlow N. Higinbotham (seated facing, right of center), president, World's Columbian Exposition.

Posing are members of the World's Columbian Exposition staff (left to right): Daniel H. Burnham, director of works; George B. Post, architect of the Manufacturers and Liberal Arts Building; M. B. Pickett, secretary of works; Richard Van Brunt, co-architect of the Electricity Building; Francis D. Millet, director of decoration; Maitland Armstrong, artist; Colonel Edmund Rice, commandant of Columbian Guard; Augustus St. Gaudens, advisor on sculpture; Henry Sargent Codman, landscape architect; George W. Maynard, muralist for the Agriculture Building; Charles F. McKim, architect of the Agriculture Building; Ernest R. Graham, assistant director of works; and Dion Geraldine, general superintendent.

Electric lights, which would become a signature feature of the world's fair, illuminated State Street at night during the dedication festivities, contributing to the feeling of pride and patriotism that Chicagoans shared.

Tens of thousands of Chicagoans crammed into the as yet unfinished Manufacturers and Liberal Arts Building for the October 21st dedication ceremony. The audience was entranced as a 5,000-person chorus performed the "Columbian Hymn" and accompanied an oration of Harriet Monroe's "Columbian Ode."

On May 1, 1893, approximately 200,000 people assembled in Jackson Park for the official opening of the World's Columbian Exposition. President Grover Cleveland, shown standing in front of the Administration Building, pressed an electric key that started the water fountains and opened the fair, although many areas remained unfinished.

The Illinois Central Railroad offered special world's fair service every five to ten minutes from the Van Buren Street pier to the exposition ground for a fare of 10 cents each way. The Illinois Central claimed they could handle 50,000 passengers an hour. The bridge across the tracks connected to the pier for steamship connections.

The Peristyle's east facade was built along Lake Michigan. Designed by Charles Atwood, it was 500 feet long and 150 feet high with a triumphal arch in its center. The Park Haven Pier, which stood at the south end of the Peristyle and jutted almost half a mile east into the lake, was one of the key points of arrival for visitors traveling to the fairgrounds by steamship.

BEAUTY AND GRANDEUR UNRIVALED

The 48 columns of the Peristyle represented the American states and territories. Topping the arch and facing west stood the *Columbus Quadriga,* a heroic sculpture by Daniel Chester French and Edward C. Potter that depicted Columbus standing in a chariot with four horses led by women. The Temple of Vesta, which sold chocolate bonbons, is at left.

The arch of the Peristyle served as a gateway to the fair and a physical link between the exposition's waterways and Lake Michigan, a symbolic gesture to Columbus's voyage.

The Great Basin was the center of the Court of Honor. The uniformly scaled and classically inspired buildings were designed in relationship to each other, creating a balanced, harmonious, and orderly arrangement of architecture. For many Americans who typically lived in towns and cities built haphazardly, the Court of Honor was their first encounter with a powerfully designed grouping of structures, and they were stunned.

The Agriculture Building fronted nearly the entire length of the Great Basin on the south. Designed by the New York firm McKim, Mead & White, it measured 500 by 800 feet. Featuring Diana, the goddess of the hunt, on its dome, the Agriculture Building was the only structure at the fair that was systematically designed in one architectural style—Roman.

The Columbian Fountain was illuminated by electric lights at night and flanked by two smaller
electric fountains at the northwest and southwest corners of the Great Basin. According to the Official
Directory, the fountain would, at times, "spout an iridescent deluge."

The Machinery Building stands southwest across the Great Basin. The main structure, which fronted the South Canal, was 842 by 492 feet; the annex was 551 by 490 feet.

The Obelisk, guarded by four lion sculptures by M. A. Waagen, served as a convenient landmark for the Colonnade, which connected the Agriculture and Machinery buildings and served as the gateway to the livestock pavilion.

The southwest corner of the Manufacturers and Liberal Arts Building is seen with one of the electric fountains in the foreground. Designed by New York architect George B. Post in the Corinthian style, the structure measured 1,687 by 787 feet, the world's largest roofed building ever constructed up to that time.

The park area behind the Administration Building was a pleasant transition space between the Court of Honor and the Terminal Station. The sign displayed on the booth to the right advertises spring water.

Seen from the bridge across the North Canal, the Administration Building boasts a majestic facade. Designed by noted American architect Richard Morris Hunt, the structure featured a golden dome, a complement to the gilded statue of the *Republic* standing opposite at the east end of the Great Basin.

The balcony surrounding the dome of the Administration Building offered impressive east and west views, including a view of the massive Ferris wheel. Artist Carl Bitter created the sculptures surrounding the domes on the balcony.

x

42

The Mines and Mining Building is visible looking south from the Lagoon. Designed by Chicago architect Solon S. Beman, the structure's dimensions were 700 by 350 feet. Beman also designed the Merchant Tailor Building at the fair.

The Manufacturers and Liberal Arts Building hides behind the Rose Garden on the Wooded Island. Sixteen acres in area, the Wooded Island was an outdoor horticulture exhibit featuring Darwin tulips, roses, climbing plants, trees, and shrubs.

The Wooded Island and the Lagoon area created a different visual and emotional experience for exposition visitors. The relationship of architecture to nature was the most important design aspect for this area of the fairgrounds, and the floral and vegetation arrangements framed the view of the buildings.

Visitors viewed the buildings surrounding the Court of Honor, such as the Electricity Building shown here, differently when they observed them from the Lagoon and the Wooded Island.

The Golden Door of the Transportation Building and its mirror reflection are seen in the Lagoon waters. The Lagoon was especially effective as a reflective surface, which further emphasized the visual merging of nature and architecture. To the left of the door is a sign advertising an Apollo Club performance at the Festival Hall.

The Horticulture Building designed by Chicago architects William LeBaron Jenney and William B. Mundie presented a magnificent 1,000-foot-long front along the Lagoon opposite the Wooded Island. This view from the Manufacturers and Liberal Arts Building shows the fairgrounds in relationship to Hyde Park and the Midway.

The Fisheries Building included a central structure and two smaller polygonal structures connected by arcades. The columns of the facade were covered with fish, and their capitals featured thousands of marine life forms.

The U.S. Government Building, with its distinctive high dome, stood between the Fisheries and the Manufacturers and Liberal Arts buildings. Designed by treasury department supervising architect Willoughby J. Edbrooke, the building was criticized for being ostentatious and for its non-classical design elements.

The artillery placed in front of the U.S. Government Building was a clue to America's imperialistic aims that would become evident to the world within five years.

Sophia G. Hayden of Boston, one of only three women recognized as architects in the nation, won the competition to design the Woman's Building. Critics considered the Woman's Building, the smallest of the primary exhibition halls on the grounds (its dimensions were 388 by 199 feet), a modest architectural success.

The loggia of the Woman's Building faces the Lagoon. Alice Rideout created the sculptural groupings that decorated the building.

The Illinois Building was the largest state structure on the grounds, and also called the most pretentious. Designed by Chicago architect W. W. Boyington & Company at a cost of $250,000, the building housed exhibits about the state and served as the headquarters for the Illinois commission.

Chicago architect Charles Atwood designed the Forestry Building. Constructed of wood with a colonnade made of tree trunks from every state in America, the Forestry Building was 528 by 208 feet and was located at the south end of the exposition grounds along the lakefront.

Steps from the North Pond led to the Fine Arts Building. Critics lauded the building's design as the best architecture on the grounds.

This view faces north along the lakefront toward the naval exhibit, with the Manufacturers and Liberal Arts Building on the left.

Pedestrians and tents dot the fairgrounds as seen from the U.S. Government Building, which looks toward the North Inlet and the foreign buildings area. The outdoor displays include a parade ground, a weather bureau, a naval observatory, a life-saving station, a lighthouse, and the battleship *Illinois*.

The Great Britain Building, called Victoria House, was an example of a typical half-timber country home from the Elizabethan period. The interior design copied elements from other well-known country homes, and the monogram *VR*, for Queen Victoria, was found throughout the building. In front of the building is *America*, a replica of a statue at the Albert Memorial in Hyde Park, London, part of a group of statues representing various regions of the world.

The Swedish Government Building was located north of the Fisheries Building on its east side.
Designed in the spirit of Sweden's churches and gentlemen houses of the sixteenth and seventeenth
centuries, the building follows the nation's tradition of covering the roof and sides with wooden
shingles.

Norway's national building, by architect W. Hansteen, was based on the stave churches the Vikings built when they converted to Christianity. The electric light in front was illuminated by Westinghouse, who outbid General Electric as supplier of electricity for the fair.

According to activist Ida B. Wells, the Haitian Building became the chosen gathering spot for African Americans who visited the fair, and it also attracted white Americans seeking an audience with Frederick Douglass, U.S. minister to Haiti and the country's chosen commissioner for the fair.

The foreign buildings from Asia generated great excitement among fair visitors. The Ceylon Building, built by native workmen, was inspired by the nation's ancient temple architecture and featured satinwood framework, ornamental scrollwork, and the characteristic large projecting eaves and hammered brass finial.

Facing the lakefront, the German Building was an eclectic melding of Gothic, German Renaissance, and modern design by Düsseldorf architect Johannes Radke. The German Building, the Krupp exhibit, and the German Village on the Midway gave Germany the dominant foreign presence on the exposition grounds.

The French Building, designed by Henri Motte and Adrien Dubisson in the French Renaissance style, occupied a site along the lakefront just east of the Fine Arts Building.

Many of the state buildings served only as headquarters for state commissions, but some also presented impressive exhibits for viewing. The cactus plantings were the most distinctive feature of the building that the territories of Arizona, Oklahoma, and New Mexico shared.

Second only to the Illinois Building in scale, the California Building was designed by San Francisco architect A. Page Brown in the style of the Spanish missions of the state. A simple whitewashed interior and exterior (purposely seamed and cracked to simulate age) and a red-tile roof, shown in this view of the south end of the building, gave the structure its distinctive character. The elevated train station is on the left.

Manufacturers and distributors used every device possible to attract attention to their displays and set them apart from the other exhibits and the millions of items on view. S. L. Allen & Co. of Philadelphia employed a rotating globe to display its planters and cultivators in the Agriculture Building.

A World of Goods and Astonishment

This Swift and Company refrigerated rail car was elaborately decked out as a display case to extol the virtues of shipping meat cross-country. A column with an Ionic capital on the left serves as a pediment for a statue of a sheep, and displays of stacked tins of meat are in the background.

The barn-like structure of the Agriculture Building was perfect for housing the multitude of food products, farm implements, and agricultural items, which were organized and displayed according to groups, classes, and nations. Visitors were fascinated by the eleven-ton block of cheese housed here— the "Mammoth Cheese"—that was imported from Canada.

The main clock tower of the Danish pavilion rises 90 feet in the south quarter of the Manufacturers and Liberal Arts Building. The scale of the building interior was immense; exposition publicity claimed that the standing army of Russia could mobilize under its roof.

The German pavilion featured an elaborate display in the Manufacturers and Liberal Arts Building. Wrought-iron gates made by the Armbruester Brothers of Frankfurt am Main led off of Columbia Avenue into the exhibits.

The Tiffany exhibit in the Manufacturers and Liberal Arts Building was considered the highlight of the American pavilion. More than 1.4 million people visited the Romanesque chapel on display.

The Japanese pavilion on Columbia Avenue was located between the Austrian and American exhibits in the north half of the Manufacturers and Liberal Arts Building.

The Edison Tower of Light, a column 30 feet in diameter covered with thousands of incandescent lights and rising 78 feet, dominated the interior of the Electricity Building.

Western Electric Company's Scenic Theatre, located in the southeast corner of the Electricity Building, was a great favorite among fairgoers. Featuring seating for an audience of 175, the theater used incandescent lighting to reveal theatrical effects by simulating the light transitions that take place over one day.

This photograph of the Mines and Mining Building interior was taken looking north toward the obelisk. The main thoroughfare running the length of the structure, called Bullion Boulevard, divided the foreign displays on the west side (left) from the domestic displays on the east side (right).

An overabundance of signs greeted visitors at the entrance to the Mammoth Crystal Cave in the Horticulture Building. This reproduction attraction, which required an additional 10-cent entrance fee, was meant to simulate the famous cave near Deadwood, South Dakota.

The Transportation Building interior walls were lined with rose-style windows.

The *Pioneer* locomotive was on exhibit in the annex attached to the Transportation Building. The *Pioneer,* manufactured by Baldwin Locomotive Works, arrived in Chicago in 1848 and was the first railroad locomotive to operate in the city, running on the Galena and Chicago Union Railroad.

European sculptures were placed on display in the East Court of the Fine Arts Building, which faced east. Great Britain was third behind France and the United States in the amount of space allocated for its art displays.

This portrait of Mrs. Bertha Honoré Palmer was displayed in the Assembly Hall of the Woman's Building. The Board of Lady Managers commissioned celebrated artist Anders L. Zorn to paint this portrait of the president of the board to honor her many efforts on behalf of women.

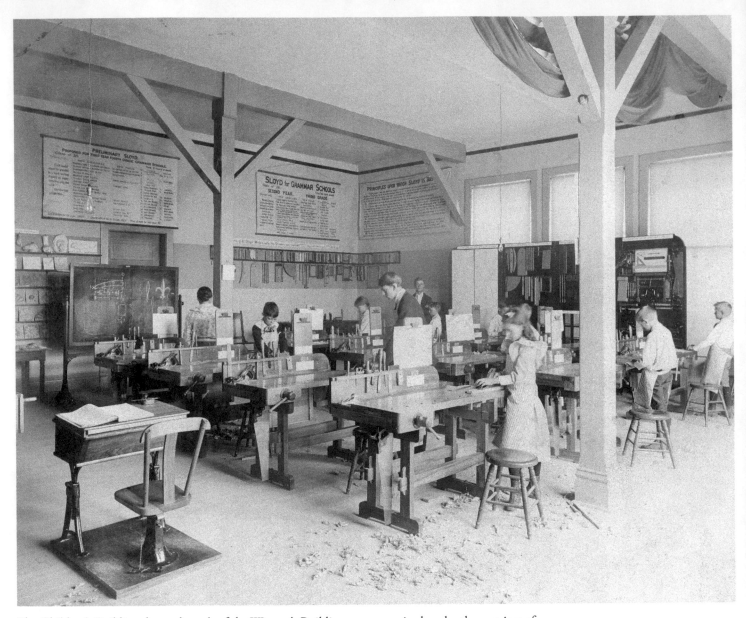

The Children's Building, located south of the Woman's Building, was organized under the auspices of the Board of Lady Managers. Focusing on the education of children, the Children's Building featured a sloyd wood shop, representing a Swedish educational system structured on handicraft-based learning.

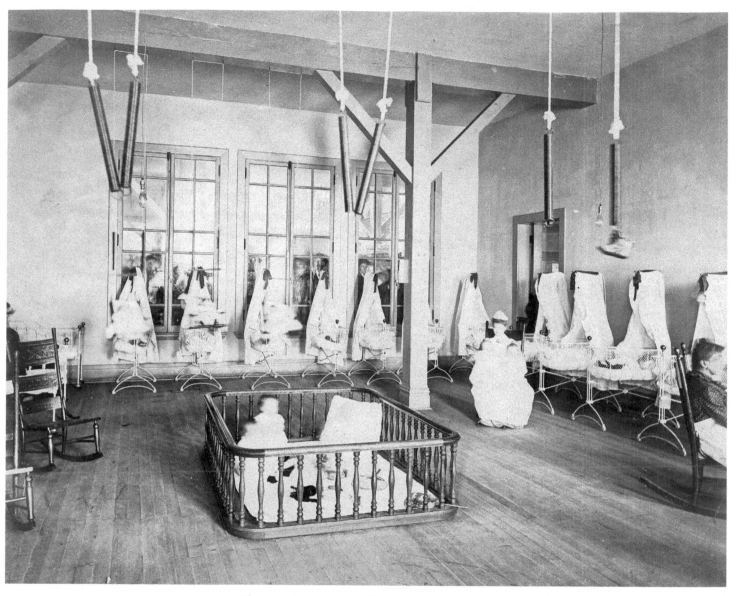

The model crèche in the Children's Building demonstrated the most modern environment and methods for raising infants.

At the south end of the U.S. Government Building, the Smithsonian Institution and the United States National Museum displayed artifacts and specimens from their anthropological and natural history collections. Visitors in the hall pause to sit on benches and view the exhibit.

The Utah Building stood at the northern extreme of the fairgrounds next to the Montana Building. Its exterior was designed to simulate various stones from the state, and the interior served both as headquarters for the territory commissioners and as a home away from home for visitors from Utah.

As part of the ethnological exhibit, Native Americans encamped in their indigenous living structures, such as these Penobscot wigwams, along the eastern edge of the South Pond. The masts and rigging of the whaling bark *Progress* are visible in the background.

The Esquimaux Village, which was inhabited by about 60 Inuits, was located in the northwest corner of the fairgrounds behind the Nebraska and North Dakota buildings and consisted of bark huts. The organizing concessionaire required the Inuits to wear their fur coats during the hot summer months.

The Japanese Tea House, which was located in the northeastern area of the Wooded Island next to the Café De Marine, required separate admission and offered light lunches and tea.

This 1831 replica of the *DeWitt Clinton* locomotive and passenger cars, which were used on the Mohawk and Hudson Railroad, was displayed outside the annex of the Transportation Building as a historical contrast to the examples of contemporary steam engines.

The *Viking*, a replica of the ancient Viking ship *Gokstad*, which had been excavated in 1880, was built in Norway and sailed from Bergen to New York, then on to Chicago via the Erie Canal and the Great Lakes. The ship was moored in the naval exhibit area near the battleship *Illinois*.

The battleship replica *Illinois* appeared to be an actual naval vessel. Built on a foundation of brick and concrete, the 348-foot-long ship featured all the fittings of an actual ship, including anchors, guns, turrets, torpedo tubes, awnings, crow's nest, and booms.

This view looking northwest to the Administration Building shows the French colonies buildings (foreground) and the windmill display. Over 15 windmill companies were featured in the commercial display, with one Dutch windmill that ground cocoa at the fair.

EXHILARATING CHAOS ON THE MIDWAY

Michigan cadets march west on the Midway past the Old Vienna complex (left) with the Captive Balloon (right) in the distance. The Midway Plaisance featured daily events to attract visitors.

Looking east toward the Midway from the Woman's Building, the Illinois Central Railroad tracks are visible in the foreground, and the Ferris wheel is in the background. Hagenbeck's Zoological Arena Company building, where Karl Hagenbeck trained animals to sell to circuses, is also seen in the distance.

The Irish Village and Blarney Castle were part of a national presentation of Irish culture, industries, and traditions that appealed to the many Americans of Irish descent. A piece of the genuine Blarney Stone, music, food, and a re-creation of Donegal Castle were featured.

The village store was typical of the thatched-roof stone buildings in the Irish Industries section at the southeast corner of the Midway. Lace makers, weavers, and butter and cheese makers demonstrated their crafts in the village area, and each visitor was presented with a genuine piece of sod from Ireland.

The prominent German presence on the main fairgrounds was reinforced on the Midway. The German Village, located between the Javanese area on the east and the Streets of Cairo on the west, occupied the largest space on the Midway. Visitors could rent the sedan chair to be carried around the Midway.

Crowds walk east on the Midway toward the Ferris wheel. The Chinese Theater is on the left and Old Vienna is on the right. A sign at left that reads "Do not miss the Ice Railway, the greatest novelty and attraction on the Midway" entices visitors with free admission.

This view facing north shows the eastern half of the Midway from the Ferris wheel to the Kilauea Volcano cyclorama. The mile-long strip of amusements charged extra fees on top of general admission to the fairgrounds.

A ride on the Ferris wheel offered a spectacular view of the fairgrounds and the Midway to the east. The domes of the Administration Building (right), U.S. Government Building (center), and Illinois Building (left) loom in the distance; the roof of one of the Ferris wheel cars is in the foreground.

For 25 cents admission, the Chinese Village featured a Joss house (temple), café, and theater with musical and acrobatic performances. A sign lists prices for an assortment of foods, including various meats, rice, and Chinese pudding with cream.

The dome and distinctive architecture of the Moorish Palace made it one of the most recognizable buildings on the Midway. In addition to a café and theater, the Palace offered a hodgepodge of attractions and displays, many of which were unrelated to Moorish culture and life.

Two women visitors peer warily at the Algerian Theatre, which drew mostly male patrons to view exotic dancers performing in a 1,000-seat auditorium. The theater was part of the Algerian and Tunisian Village and a repeat amusement from the 1889 Paris world's fair. Fairgoers flocked to the re-created Algerian and Tunisian streets, where, for 25 cents, you could see snake charmers, watch jugglers, hear an orchestra perform, and buy souvenirs.

The Egyptian Temple was part of the Streets of Cairo section of the Midway. Egyptian antiquities were on view inside the structure.

The Wild East show, which was a feature of the Turkish Village, featured Bedouins performing equestrian feats, including mock battles with spears and swords. This show was complemented by Buffalo Bill's Wild West show, which was not affiliated with the exposition or the Midway, but was an independent attraction near the fairgrounds. Because of its location, Buffalo Bill's show, which had been rejected from participation in the fair, took away potential exposition patrons.

Billing itself as the World's Congress of Beauty, a reference to the many legitimate international meetings on key world topics that the fair sponsored, this display of women wearing native costume sought to brand itself as an educational experience. Some visitors complained that many of the women were not from the nations they represented.

The cyclorama of the Hawaiian volcano Kilauea was housed in the largest building on the Midway, and it cost 50 cents to enter. Cycloramas, panoramic paintings inside a round or hectagonal building that were often accompanied by narration and music, had become popular urban spectacles during the late nineteenth century, and people marveled at these realistic visual illusions.

The famous German zoo director Karl Hagenbeck built a complex that included an amphitheater modeled after the Coliseum in Rome and an arena, with admission ranging from 25 cents to one dollar. Under the direction of trainer Miss Liebemich, a cast of exotic animals, including a dwarf elephant, performed unusual feats of skill—including lions riding horses, bears walking tightropes, and tigers riding velocipedes.

For visitors who missed the Paris 1889 world's fair, the Midway offered the next best thing—a 25-foot-tall model of the Eiffel Tower, complete with working elevators and lights.

A dancer pauses to pose for an amateur photographer on his way to perform in the Brazilian Music Hall.

South Sea Islanders enter the South Sea Islanders Village Theatre to perform. Over 300 people, hailing from the islands of Borneo, Fiji, Java, Jehore, New Zealand, Samoa, and Sumatra, resided in the fair's South Sea Island Village.

The crowds visiting the Midway made the exposition financially successful. The fair corporation negotiated lucrative concession agreements with Midway amusements, and the Midway became a model for organizing commercial attractionsfor all future world's fairs.

This view of the Transportation Building looks east from Hyde Park across some railroad tracks. The Columbian Exchange Hotel (right) was likely one of the many speculative ventures that developed around the fairgrounds to take advantage of the crowds visiting the exposition.

A City Beautiful

The Bureau of Public Comfort Building was located at the north-end entrance of the fairgrounds. It offered numerous amenities for visitors—including telegraph and telephone services, toilets, parlors, reading rooms, a barbershop, a coat check room, lost and found, and the sale of toiletries, stamps, stationery, and newspapers at a moderate price—and staff were on hand to provide information and directions. Some of the other large buildings on the fairgrounds also incorporated some public comfort amenities.

The three-story Café de Marine building, which stood at the northeastern edge of the Lagoon, was a popular fish restaurant. Other restaurants nearby—including the Japanese Tea House, the Swedish Restaurant, and the Polish Café—drew many hungry visitors to this area.

Cowboy, by sculptor Alexander Phimister Proctor, and its companion piece, *Indian Scout,* also by Proctor, stood along the Lagoon in front of the Transportation Building.

The *Farm Horse* by Edward C. Potter (the farmer himself was sculped by Daniel Chester French) stood along the Great Basin, with other examples of horses as well as an ox.

Attendants wait for customers to rent rolling chairs. A total of 2,500 Columbia rolling chairs were available from 21 pavilions spread across the fairgrounds. Visitors could rent a single chair with a guide pushing them for 75 cents an hour.

The Great Basin featured an electric launch landing. The Electric Launch and Navigation Company operated more than 40 electric launches at the fair. The three-mile circuit began in the Great Basin and ended in the North Pond at the landing on the south entrance of the Fine Arts Building. With a capacity of 24 passengers each, the electric launches, with their distinctive red and yellow awnings, were an ideal way to move about the fairgrounds and see the buildings.

The elevated intramural electric railway snakes through the state buildings at the north end of the fairgrounds on its way to its final stop near the Fisheries Building.

The replica of the Spanish Convent of Santa Maria de la Rabida was located on the lakeshore just east of the Agriculture Building and just south of the Casino Building. Columbus stayed at the convent while his three-ship expedition to the New World was readied at a nearby port. Fair visitors could see the most important Columbus artifacts and documents on display in the replica convent.

The interior courtyard of the Convent of Santa Maria de la Rabida, a replica of the convent where Columbus lived before his voyage to the Americas, provided a respite from the hustle and bustle and the noise of the fairgrounds.

The bandstand and concession stand were built directly in front of the Electricity Building. Bands performed popular music in daily and evening concerts in a variety of fairground settings, including these bandstands. John Philip Sousa was a popular performer at the fair.

The Park Haven Pier, which measured 250 feet wide by 2,500 feet long, featured a moveable sidewalk that looped at each end of the pier. Bands seated inside the west loop played popular music concerts.

Visitors gather along the lakeshore edge of the fairgrounds to watch the arrival of the Spanish caravels.
Hats and sunglasses helped keep the summer sun at bay.

Replicas of the Spanish caravels *Niña, Pinta,* and *Santa Maria* arrive at the exposition on July 12, 1893. The three ships dropped anchor behind the Agriculture Building and adjacent to the Convent of Santa Maria de la Rabida.

The Court of Honor is illuminated at night by electricity. The Columbian Exposition was the first electric world's fair in history. Strings of incandescent electric lights and searchlights mounted on top of buildings created an incredible nighttime spectacle for visitors, and served as a memorable demonstration of the power of electricity.

Notes on the Photographs

These notes, listed by page number, attempt to include all aspects of the photographs that are known. Each of the photographs is identified by the page number, a title or description, photographer and collection, archive, and call or box number when applicable. Although every attempt was made to collect all data, in some cases complete data may have been unavailable due to the age and condition of some of the photographs and records.

Printed in the USA
CPSIA information can be obtained
at www.ICGtesting.com
JSHW072026140824
68134JS00042B/3805

9 781683 368908